A Purcell Organ Album

SELECTED AND ARRANGED BY MARTIN SETCHELL

MUSIC DEPARTMENT

OXFORD
UNIVERSITY PRESS

OXFORD
UNIVERSITY PRESS

Great Clarendon Street, Oxford OX2 6DP, England
198 Madison Avenue, New York, NY 10016, USA

Oxford University Press is a department of the University of Oxford.
It furthers the University's aim of excellence in research, scholarship,
and education by publishing worldwide

First published 2009

5 7 9 10 8 6

ISBN 978-0-19-336569-8

Music origination by
Enigma Music Production Services, Amersham, Bucks.
Printed in Great Britain on acid-free paper by
Halstan & Co. Ltd., Amersham, Bucks.

Contents

Introduction

The memorial tablet to Henry Purcell (1659–95) in the North aisle of Westminster Abbey, London, with its moving tribute 'gone to that Blessed Place where only his Harmony can be exceeded', is testament to the esteem in which both the man and his music have been held ever since his untimely death at the age of 36.

Most of Purcell's early life, like that of his musical family, revolved around the Chapel Royal and Westminster Abbey, London, and particularly their organs. In 1673, aged 14, he became assistant to Hingeston as 'keeper, mender, maker, repairer and tuner of the regals, organs, virginals, flutes and recorders',[1] and was already copying out organ parts. In 1679 his mentor John Blow resigned his post as organist of Westminster Abbey, apparently in deference to the 20-year-old Purcell. Three years later, in 1682, the young man took Lowe's place as one of the three Chapel Royal organists,[2] and in 1683 he succeeded Hingeston as 'maker and curator of the King's organs'. He later served as a member of the King's private music, principally as a keyboardist. His career advancement as a practitioner was thus extremely fast, and reflective of his skills and talents.

Yet despite the importance of the organ, his surviving music originally written for the instrument is sparse, comprising a mere handful of pieces[3] (though it is likely he composed many more at the organ which were never written down). Even the most famous work attributed to him, the *Voluntary on the Old Hundredth*, remains of doubtful authorship, and these few voluntaries, though well crafted, hardly do justice to his versatility or genius. The huge corpus of work written during his tragically short life contains far more secular music than sacred, and as a composer he was a man of the theatre as much as a man of the church.

This volume therefore comprises a selection of pieces drawn from what I consider to be amongst his most attractive secular music and suited to organ arrangement. Most are taken from his music for the theatre, and in particular the mature works from the last decade his life: *Dido and Aeneas*, *Dioclesian*, *The Fairy Queen*, *King Arthur*, *Bonduca*, *Amphitryon*, *The Double Dealer*, *Abdelazar*, and *The Indian Queen*.

The first section comprises eight Trumpet Tunes, including the most famous one in D major and the Cibell from the harpsichord pieces. The second section is titled Airs and Dances, and brings together a wide variety of pieces. It includes examples of his gift for melody in works such as 'Fairest Isle' and 'When I am laid in earth', short gentle pieces, and some characteristic lively dance movements – hornpipe, jig, minuet, bourrée, and the famous Rondeau from *Abdelazar*. There are also two extended movements: part of the opening symphony of the 1694 birthday ode for Queen Mary, *Come ye Sons of Art*, and a Chaconne from *The Fairy Queen*.

All these are new arrangements, and cover a variety of moods and styles. Parts of some pieces have been arranged as trio textures for two manuals and pedal; other pieces are arranged for manuals only. In all, the pieces will suit a range of needs in both services and recitals.

---

[1] Peter Holman, *Purcell* (Oxford Studies of Composers) (Oxford, 1994), p. 11.

[2] E. F. Rimbault (ed.), *The Old Cheque Book or Book of Remembrance of the Chapel Royal from 1561 to 1744* (London, 1872; reprinted 1966), p. 17.

[3] See H. Purcell, *Organ Works*, ed. H. McLean (2nd edition, Novello, 1967).

As this is essentially a performing edition, markings have been deliberately kept to a minimum. Tempo markings in square brackets and all metronome marks, dynamics, and registration indications are editorial suggestions only and may be varied if desired. Ornamentation has mostly been reduced to the simple marking *tr*, with the trill played on the beat, starting on the note above. Additional ornamentation, like discreet decoration of repeats of a melodic phrase, is at the player's discretion. Movements scored for manuals only may be played with pedals if desired, and conversely some movements or sections with pedal can be satisfactorily rendered by manuals only. The many binary form movements can be extended to suit by repeating sections as required. Marks of articulation have been kept to a minimum; on occasion, a comma above the stave has been used to indicate the end of a phrase. As a general rule, articulation in most of these pieces should be light and detached, reflecting their origin as dance movements.

It is my hope that both church and concert organists will find some useful additions to their repertoire in this compendium volume, and that it will encourage them and their listeners to enjoy a wider range of Henry Purcell's delightful music in this, and beyond, the 350th anniversary year of his birth.

MARTIN SETCHELL
Christchurch, New Zealand
2009

Symphony to Act V
from *The Fairy Queen*

HENRY PURCELL
arr. Martin Setchell

Trumpet Air
from *The Indian Queen*

HENRY PURCELL
arr. Martin Setchell

Trumpet Tune: Act V Consort

from *King Arthur*

HENRY PURCELL
arr. Martin Setchell

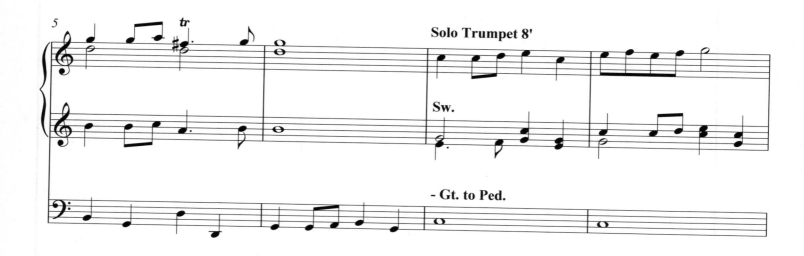

Trumpet Tune

from *Dioclesian*

HENRY PURCELL
arr. Martin Setchell

Trumpet Tune

HENRY PURCELL
arr. Martin Setchell

Repeat bars 1–4 followed by bars 17–24 if desired.

Trumpet Tune, called the Cibell

HENRY PURCELL
arr. Martin Setchell

2nd time: **poco rit.**

Trumpet Tune: Warlike Consort

from *King Arthur*

HENRY PURCELL
arr. Martin Setchell

Trumpet Tune
from *The Indian Queen*

HENRY PURCELL
arr. Martin Setchell

Symphony and Chorus

from *Come ye Sons of Art*

HENRY PURCELL
arr. Martin Setchell

Solo Trumpet

If love's a sweet passion

from *The Fairy Queen*

HENRY PURCELL
arr. Martin Setchell

How blest are shepherds
from *King Arthur*

HENRY PURCELL
arr. Martin Setchell

Shepherd, shepherd leave decoying

from *King Arthur*

HENRY PURCELL
arr. Martin Setchell

Fairest Isle

from *King Arthur*

HENRY PURCELL
arr. Martin Setchell

When I am laid in earth

from Dido and Aeneas

HENRY PURCELL
arr. Martin Setchell

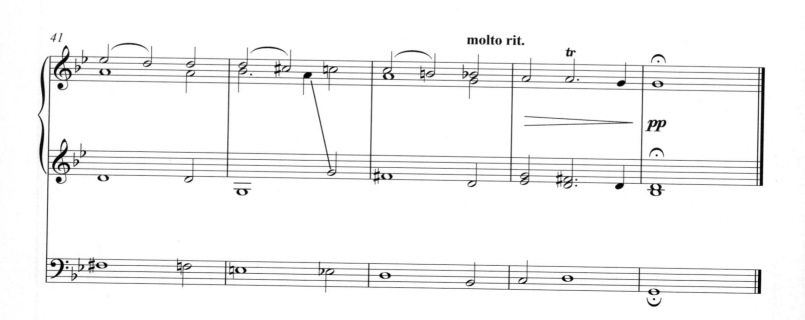

Air
from *King Arthur*

HENRY PURCELL
arr. Martin Setchell

Here's the summer, sprightly, gay

from *The Fairy Queen*

HENRY PURCELL
arr. Martin Setchell

Hornpipe

from *Amphitryon*

HENRY PURCELL
arr. Martin Setchell

Bourrée

from *Amphitryon*

HENRY PURCELL
arr. Martin Setchell

MANUAL

Third Act Tune: Rondeau

from *Abdelazar*

HENRY PURCELL
arr. Martin Setchell

Minuett
from *The Double Dealer*

HENRY PURCELL
arr. Martin Setchell

Aire: Second Music

from Bonduca

HENRY PURCELL
arr. Martin Setchell

Round thy coast

from *King Arthur*

HENRY PURCELL
arr. Martin Setchell

[Andante]

MANUAL

mp **8' 4' Flutes** (*repeat 8'*)

poco rit. (2nd time)

Second Act Tune: Air

from *The Fairy Queen*

HENRY PURCELL
arr. Martin Setchell

First Act Tune: Jig

from *The Fairy Queen*

HENRY PURCELL
arr. Martin Setchell

Dance for the Fairies

from *The Fairy Queen*

HENRY PURCELL
arr. Martin Setchell

Rondeau

from *The Fairy Queen*

HENRY PURCELL
arr. Martin Setchell

D. C. al Fine

Chaconne: Dance for Chinese Man and Woman

from *The Fairy Queen*

HENRY PURCELL
arr. Martin Setchell

56

Variation 3